Love, Hurt, and Everything Above

Bo Vang

Love, Hurt, and Everything Above © 2022
Bo Vang

All rights reserved.

No part of this publication may be reproduced, stored in a retrieval system, or transmitted, in any form or by any means, electronic, mechanical, photocopying, recording or otherwise, without the prior written permission of the presenters.

Bo Vang asserts the moral right to be identified as author of this work.

Presentation by *BookLeaf Publishing*

Web: www.bookleafpub.com

E-mail: info@bookleafpub.com

ISBN: 9789357614955

First edition 2022

I would like to dedicate this book of poetry
to my family for always being there for me.
And for those who are in love and those
who are hurting. We are all in this together.

ACKNOWLEDGEMENT

I want to acknowledge my family who supports me and gives me the strength never to give up.

I Think It's Love

Like the leaves flowing through the wind,
like the rainbow that comes after the rain,
You are my harmony.

When the wind echoes through the night, I hear
your name.
When the rain touches my skin, I feel your love.
You are the beat to my heart.

Like the sunshine blanketing its warmth over
earth,
like the butterfly kissing each delicate flower,
You complete me.

There is not a day that goes by that I don't think
of you.
You're stuck to me like peanut butter and jelly.
You are my unison.

You continued to surprise me with your sweet
self,
always making sure that I continue to smile.
You are my honeybee.

Even though this is so tacky
and I am a hopeless romantic,
You are my cheesy love poem.

Spring is in the Air

Your love sends a cool
gentle breeze that brushes me
like the cherry blossoms
drifting in the wind.

Your love absorbs into me
like the rainwater being soaked
into a dry flower
in the Spring season.

Your love cradles me
like the sun's ray
beaming down on my body
on a warm Spring day.

Your love is as soft
as the blooming flowers
that flushed its pink tones
like the colors of my cheeks.

It's silly, really

Come take my hand and don't let go.
Promise me that this will last forever,
promise me that this is not a dream.
I waited so long to find this pure feeling,
so long have I waited to be held like this.
The night closes in on us, leaving
the outside world going silent.
It's just us.
You and me.

Dancing our night away,
feeling free like a cherry blossom
drifting through the strong winds.
The silly sensation growing inside of me,
causing me to smile at the starry night sky.
The moment we both said "I do",
I can finally say,
I found you.
I found you.

A Twinkling Star

Although you may not see it,
you're like a cup of stars.
You fill me up with your brightness,
when things turn dark in my world.
Just a small dose of happiness is all I need.
Your sparks of flare warm my cooling heart.
In my darkest moments,
when I am sad and scared,
your light soaks into me,
covering me until I am
embedded with your love.
I cannot thank you enough,
as your light shines through.
In the corners of my mind, your existing
luminosity guides me out of the dark,
pulling me through until I can find life again.
One sip of you can make me feel radiant.
Just one full cup of your love will satisfy me.

One More Time

The way that I bloomed is all because of you
I can feel the butterflies kissing me from inside
My knees tremble when I'm in your embrace
Your presence sends me high up to the clouds
And I could go on and on, letting the world
know how much you mean to me.

Dance

Your hands on my waist,
through my hair,
thinking about
when you touched me there.
Closing my eyes,
here you are,
we are dancing in the dark.

Kiss Me

He said "Kiss me, my lips yearn for you,
you are the one for me, which is true."
He said, "Kiss me under this shady tree,
there's no one in this world
except for you and me."
He said, "Kiss me as passionately as you can.
You know you're my girl and I'm your man."
He said, "Kiss me beneath this starry sky.
When our lips touch each other,
it feels like we can fly."
He said, "Kiss me.
Our love will show us our way.
You are my light and I am yours,
always."
He said, "Kiss me, together we can be.
Lost in our little world,
it's only you and me."
He said, "Kiss me, and I'll never let you go.
I'll hold you tight, I'll hold you near,
I'll love you forever that I know."

Sky

You're like the night sky,
hard to make out,
yet so beautiful in the light of the moon,
mysterious and astonishing,
not fully understood,
yet always looked at with curious eyes,
filled with beauty and mystery.

You're like the morning sun in the sky,
warming and welcoming,
beautiful yet hard to stare at,
shining with compassion,
and missed while not there.

You're like the rain,
calm, and gentle,
loved by most,
cool to the touch,
and so amazing and wonderful.

You've always been wonderful,
and I love you dearly,
you make me smile when I wish to frown,
when all seems lost,
I look upon your face,
and no matter what,

all hope returns in the blink of an eye,
your smile is intoxicated,
and quite frankly,
everything about you is one word,
PERFECT,
and no matter what anyone says,
I will always love you and keep you close
to my heart.

No Matter What

Your gentle heart,
and soft-spoken words
fill me with a feeling unlike any other.
Your handsomeness
stuns me,
your smile
hypnotizes me,
your every being
fills me with love.
I can't help it,
no matter how much I try,
you pull me in,
unable to escape,
I keep falling deeper and deeper
in love with you.
I'm afraid there's no end to it,
you always find a way to make me smile,
no matter how sad I am,
I'm just happy to know I have you,
and I never want to change that.
I'll just let you know,
no matter what happens,
I'll always be by your side,
because honestly,
I love you no matter what.

High-five

That bristly touch.
That warm feeling.
That strong grip.
Those blistered knuckles.
Those talented fingers.
His hands aren't always perfect
but I love them.

Hold on Tight

When he looks into your eyes and stares at you
for a while and smiles,
when he gently caresses his hands with yours,
when his cool fingers touch your face,
when he softly plants his kisses on your lips,
when he pulls you in to deepen the kiss and
everything
just seems so weightless like floating in the
water;
that's when you know you got someone special.

Yes, I do!

Do you hate me?
No, I don't hate you.
I hate what you did though.
You lied to me until
the guilt ate you inside.
I hate that I can't get over you.
I'm still in love with you
like it was the first time
we laid eyes on each other.
I hate that you are so blind,
not seeing how much pain you have caused me.
Every night, I cry myself to sleep,
hoping that it was all just a nightmare,
a nightmare that I wish to never enter.
I hate that you used me.
You made me believed that we were in love.
You used me to boost your confidence.
When no one else loved you, I did.
I hate that you are so heartless,
disregarding my feelings like an unwanted letter.
Never seeing eye to eye with me,
like a random stranger walking by.
And if you were to ask again,

Yes, I do hate you.

Falling Hard

You can't hurt me because I already saw it coming. But why is it so hard to stop loving you? It feels like a thousand needles piercing into my heart. One by one it penetrates in, slowly piercing through each layer. Congratulations, you fucken did it. You broke it even when you said that you wouldn't. This continuous stabbing makes it so much harder to breathe. Each taking breath feels like a clogged straw, trying to gasp for air, and for that, I can no longer breathe anymore.

The pain collects at the bottom of my eyes, waiting to pour out into sadness. A sorrow builds up at the edge of my throat, quivering away as I tremble. No words can come out. All I could do is scream like a crying banshee, wailing in misery. If I can't let you go, can you? Let me go because you knew that you can no longer make me happy. Let me go so that you will realize you made the mistake. I just want to fall in love again, but not when my heart is aching. So, let me go. Just let me go.

Again

Too many times have I let myself go
into that miserable state.
There's this constant cycle that I am in.
I am sucked into this vortex,
circling around and around,
a never-ending loop.
It suffocates me.
It embraces me, latching on like a hungry leech.
I'm tired, and yet it repeats itself.

You are the Prince of Darkness,
the same evil that I have come upon again.
The same devil but in a different vessel.
Have you had enough?
I sure have and yet I am stuck in this trance.
You tease me with your grin.
You haunt me with your looks.
You trigger me with your touch.
You pull me without gravity,
and here I am, in this whirlwind of misery,
repeating itself once again.

Broken

I can't breathe whenever you're around.
It feels like a clogged straw, difficult to take in
life.
      It's hard
      It's hard
There's a sudden urgency waiting to escape from
my eyes,
waiting to spill and let out my story.
I can't
I can't
I'm silenced by your hands.
I'm stopped by your words.
      I'm done
      I'm done
Your eyes hold a grip on me
And once again, I am surrounded by the
darkness
      I'm lost
      I'm lost
This isn't love, this is hatred
This isn't you, this is the devil
      I've fallen
      So deep inside this vortex
      The weight of my regret drags me in
      I'm forever gone

No More

You didn't mean to hurt me,
but you did.
I just want to be able to
let you go and never put myself
in that situation ever again.

I Hate Myself

Some days I am fine
Some days I tell myself to get over it
Some days I feel lost
Some days I feel so used
Some days I tell myself that I am a fool
Some days I cry because I realized
how horrible you are
And yet, here I am, still so much
in love with you
So in love that I hate myself for it

Conceal

I add another layer around my lips to cover up,
making sure that it isn't visible to others.
I open my makeup drawer,
trying to decide which shade to wear today.
A shy shade?
A secretive one?
A happy color?

Which one to wear?

Maybe I will go with the dark red wine tint,
a shade so beautiful in the eyes of others,
but to me, all I see is a haunting memory of pain.
Applying a layer of sorrow,
going over and over on my lips.
When I smack my lips together,
I can taste the bitterness of his love,
the saltiness of my regret.
The regret of letting him take over me.
A sharp tear causes the color to bleed out,
trailing down my lips,
the deep pigment streaming down,
looking like dark red wine.

Me First

I deserve to be chosen, not considered
I am a priority, not a choice
And if you have to hesitate on choosing me,
Then move along and go about your way
because you already made the decision
to not choose me first.

An Apology

I'm sorry pillow for all of the tears you collected.
I'm sorry heart for all of the scars I inflicted on
you.
I'm sorry brain for all of the painful memories
you made.
I'm sorry to myself for causing so much pain.

Don't make me fall in love with you if you can't
love me.

Another One

I looked at you and smiled.
Not because of what you did
or how you broke me,
but because you're another
collection for my poetry.

Printed in the USA
CPSIA information can be obtained
at www.ICGtesting.com
LVHW021003141223
766083LV00087B/1825

9 789357 614955